TIME-TRAVEL GUIDES

The ANCIENT GREEKS

SARAH RIDLEY

Gareth Stevens PUBLISHING

Please visit our website,
www.garethstevens.com.
For a free color catalog of all
our high-quality books, call
toll free 1-800-542-2595 or
fax 1-877-542-2596.

Cataloging-in-Publication Data

Names: Ridley, Sarah, 1963-, author.
Title: The Ancient Greeks / Sarah Ridley.
Description: Buffalo, NY : Gareth Stevens Publishing, 2026. | Series: Time-travel guides | Includes glossary and index.
Identifiers: ISBN 9781482475425 (pbk.) | ISBN 9781482475432 (library bound) | ISBN 9781482475449 (ebook)
Subjects: LCSH: Greece--Civilization--Juvenile literature. | Greece--History--Juvenile literature. | Greece--Social life and customs--Juvenile literature.
Classification: LCC DF741.R533 2026 | DDC 938--dc23

Published in 2026 by
Gareth Stevens Publishing
2544 Clinton St.
Buffalo, NY 14224

First published in Great Britain in 2022 by Hodder & Stoughton

Artwork and Design: Collaborate Agency
Editor: Sarah Silver

Picture credits:
p.4-5: © johnbraid/Shutterstock.com, p.28: © Vincenzo Iacovoni/Shutterstock.com,

Printed in China
CPSIA compliance information: Batch #QW26GS: For further information contact Gareth Stevens at 1-800-542-2595.

CONTENTS

Athens	4
Putting Athens on the map	6
Arrive by boat	8
Where to stay	10
Enjoy a symposium (men and boys only)	12
Visit the gynaikon (women and girls only)	14
Visit the Acropolis	16
See an assembly	18
Time to exercise!	20
Go shopping	22
Visit a pottery workshop	24
Enjoy the theater	26
Visit quick!	28
Glossary	30
Further information	31
Index	32

ATHENS

Welcome to Athens. Between the years 479–323 BCE, Athens was one of the most important cities in the world. Together with other Greek city-states, such as Sparta, Corinth, and Olympia, it made up the ancient Greek world.

Shown here in the 21st century, Athens is the capital of modern Greece. Today, you can still visit some buildings dating back to the time of the ancient Greeks. Historians and archaeologists have studied these buildings, as well as other ruins, objects, and written records, to learn about the lives of the people who lived in and around ancient Athens.

TIME-TRAVEL GUIDES

Your time-travel guide

Congratulations on buying this Time-Travel Guide – the must-have companion for travelers journeying into the past. The guide will give you advice on where to stay, what to see, and how best to spend your time in Athens. Top travel tips throughout will give you the low-down on what to bring, where to shop, what to avoid and what not to miss!

Top Tip

Exchange spices for coins

Raid your kitchen and pack spices, black pepper, and salt in your bag. These foods were all highly valued by the ancient Greeks. Soon after you arrive, visit the *agora* (see pages 22–23) where you can sell these items in return for solid silver coins. You'll need coins to pay for things on your trip.

Time to go back

Now we will use time-travel technology to transport you back to visit Athens 2,500 years ago. Brace yourselves! The ancient Greeks lived very different lives from us!

PUTTING ATHENS ON THE MAP

The history of Athens began 6,000 years ago when the first inhabitants started to live on a rocky hill, now called the Acropolis. You are visiting this busy city around 450–430 BCE. It is a crowded place, full of narrow winding lanes, homes large and small, and lots of must-see places. Some of these sites are highlighted on the map below. To learn more about them, simply turn to the page numbers given in the map key.

Athens and the ancient Greek world

The city of Athens lies within Attica, the name for the land that makes up the rest of this city-state and covers an area of about 927 square miles (2,400 sq km). There are farms, trading ports, harbors, villages, towns, mountains, and wild areas.

As a time traveler, it's important to understand that ancient Greece is not a single country like Greece today. It is a collection of about 1,000 separate city-states across what we now call Greece, bits of southern Italy and Spain, and other places nearby. These city-states are at war with each other, fighting for power, although they do sometimes work together to defend against enemies, such as the Persians.

At the time you are visiting Athens, it has been rebuilt under the leadership of the Athenian statesman Pericles (c. 495–429 BCE), after the Persians destroyed much of the city.

Top Tip

Think like an ancient Greek

The ancient Greeks believe that their gods and goddesses have control over all areas of life on Earth. They pray and make offerings to whichever god or goddess they think can make good things happen, such as a safe journey or an excellent harvest, or prevent bad things from happening.

Top Tip

Who is an ancient Greek?

Most time travelers today talk about the ancient Greeks. However, that was a name given to them by the ancient Romans who came after them. The ancient Greeks call themselves *Hellenes* and their land, *Hellas*.

ARRIVE BY BOAT

The best way to reach Athens is to arrive by boat at Piraeus, the harbor a few miles from Athens. It's a very noisy, busy place. Merchant ships come and go all day long, bringing in goods and shipping them out. This is also where fishermen sail back to shore with their fresh catch of seafood.

Trade

Trade brings great wealth to Athens. Ships bring wheat and other food to feed the people of Athens, as well as spices, glass, and metal. They also carry enslaved people: men, women, and children are often captured during the many wars fought between Greek city-states.

When it's time to sail off to trade with other places, merchants load their ships with *amphorae* (jugs), clay pots filled with local goods, including honey, olive oil, and wine, as well as figs, fine pottery, and baskets of cheese.

Top Tip

Don't walk

Hire a mule and cart to transport you through the crowds to Athens. It's a long walk otherwise! The Athenians built long stone walls (the Long Walls) to protect the route between Piraeus and Athens a few years ago.

Give thanks

Start thinking like an ancient Greek by praying to Poseidon, god of the seas, to thank him for your safe voyage. Plan a visit to a temple of Poseidon, where you can pour wine or olive oil on an altar as an offering to him.

Admire the fleet

A strong navy protects Athens and Athenians from attack and also helped to build the Greek Empire. The navy uses long, slim wooden boats called *triremes*. If you are lucky (or unlucky!), you'll see 170 oarsmen rowing a trireme speedily across the harbor.

WHERE TO STAY

Luckily for you, a wealthy man you met on board your ship has invited you to stay. Like most ancient Greek homes, his is built from mud bricks and wood, around a courtyard with an altar where the family worship the gods. The upper floor has bedrooms, storerooms, and the *gynaikon* (see pages 14–15).

No soap!

Ancient Greeks like to keep clean. Most people have to use the public baths, but your host has a bathroom. Enslaved people will fill the short bath with hot water to prepare it for you. The ancient Greeks don't have soap, but rub clay and then oil on their skin and scrape it off with a long metal tool called a *strigil*.

Top Tip

No toilet!

Be warned! There are no toilets in ancient Greece. Ask to use a chamber pot if you need to go.

Nowhere to stay?

Travelers who don't know anyone in Athens can pay for a bed or a room at an inn in Piraeus or Athens. There are plenty of them, but guests would be wise to check for bedbugs before accepting the room!

Don't wander around

Men and women live quite separate lives, even in the same house. So don't go wandering around your guest's home or you may enter rooms where you are not welcome! The men of the household and male guests often spend time in the *andron* (the men's room), a beautiful room with a mosaic floor.

ENJOY A SYMPOSIUM (MEN AND BOYS ONLY)

You are extremely lucky. Your new friend has invited you to a *symposium*, the drinking party he is holding this evening in the andron. He wants to introduce you to his friends. (You will only receive this invitation if you are male.)

The host decides

The wine and water are mixed in a large bowl called a *krater* and served to guests in a wide, shared drinking cup called a *kylix*. Your host decides he doesn't want a rowdy party, so he tells the enslaved boys serving the wine to add plenty of water to make the wine weak!

Top Tip

Pass the kylix

Take care, as it is quite easy to spill wine from a kylix. It's not easy to hold it steady when you are lying down on a couch, propped up on your arm. Usually only the right hand was used for eating and drinking.

Food and entertainment

You won't go hungry. Dinner is served before the drinking begins. You will be offered plates of tasty snacks, such as bread, olives, or slices of meat. Enjoy listening to the stories of the other guests and tell a few of your own, while female musicians and dancers also keep you entertained.

VISIT THE GYNAIKON (WOMEN AND GIRLS ONLY)

As a female guest, you'll spend time with the women of the household. Climb the stairs to the *gynaikon*, the room where women, children, and their nurses spend most of their time.

Raising children

Young children in a wealthy household have plenty of wooden and clay toys to play with. It's the job of the mother and grandmother to teach older girls how to spin, weave, and run a household. Boys are taught to read, write, and do math, first by a teacher and then at the *gymnasium* (see pages 20–21).

Top Tip

Put on a tunic

Ask one of the women to show you how to fold, belt, and pin your tunic. One type is called a *peplos* (see far right) and is made from one long piece of woven cloth, but when belted looks like a skirt and a top!

Top Tip

Visit Sparta!

Make time to visit the city-state of Sparta, where some people say that women are treated more equally. Girls are taught to read, do math, and keep fit.

Spinning and weaving

Prepare to get crafty. Women spin wool or flax into thread and weave the threads into cloth on looms. Listen to the women chatting about friends and family while they weave. They also plan the day's meals, decide what food needs to be bought from the market and give orders to the enslaved people who do all the harder work in the home.

Women's lives

Wealthy women are comfortable, but they don't have much control over their lives. As girls they had to obey their father, and as women they obey their husbands. They are not allowed to vote (see pages 18–19) or go to a law court. In poorer families, women work on the farm or in the family workshop while raising children and running the home. Enslaved women work all the time!

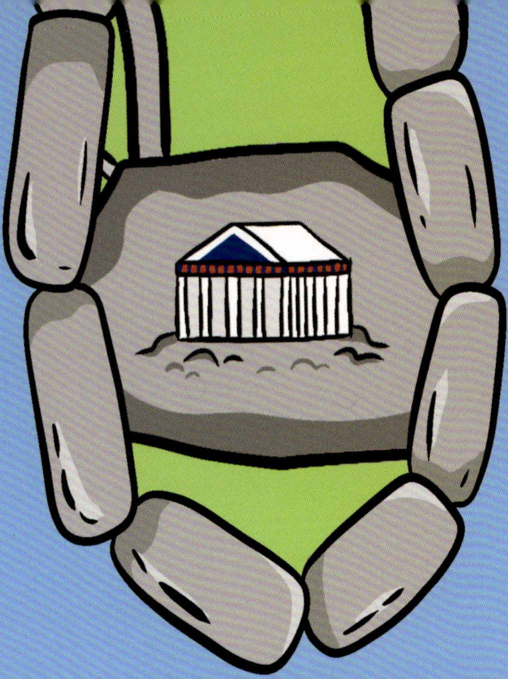

VISIT THE ACROPOLIS

After a breakfast of porridge, head for the Acropolis. You can't miss this sacred hill, high above the city. It's a steep climb, so wear cool clothes and start out early. As you enter the gates, be amazed by the many temples and statues. Most of these are dedicated to Athena, goddess of war and wisdom. She is believed to give special protection to Athens.

Top Tip

See the statue

Only a handful of priests and priestesses are allowed inside the Parthenon. Get as close as you can to an open doorway to catch sight of the 40-foot- (12 m) tall, ivory and gold statue of Athena inside. The statue cost more than it took to build the rest of the Parthenon!

Admire it

The Parthenon is the largest temple on the Acropolis. Gleaming white marble columns surround the temple. Look up to admire the sculptures of Greek gods and goddesses high above you. Walk around the whole building to follow the colorful procession of people and animals shown on the carved frieze. The carvings show the annual procession to the Erechtheion (Temple of Athena).

Top Tip

Take in the view

From the Acropolis you can see the city-state of Athens, where about 100,000 people live within the city walls, and take in views across the countryside and out to sea.

Look out for: the Erechtheion

Most of the buildings and statues on the Acropolis were built between 447 and 432 BCE to replace those destroyed by the Persians in 480 BCE. The Erechtheion may be smaller than the Parthenon, but it is the most important and sacred temple on the Acropolis. Each summer, on the goddess Athena's birthday, people organize a procession to bring a new dress for the wooden statue of Athena inside the temple.

SEE AN ASSEMBLY

From a distance, take the chance to watch democracy in action on a hillside near the Acropolis called the Pnyx. It's here that citizens gather about four times a month to debate and vote at the assembly. It's a crush as at least 6,000 people attend each assembly!

Who could vote?

Athens is a democracy, which means "rule by the people," but only some Athenians can take part: male citizens over the age of 20 who were born in Athens. No enslaved people, women, or foreigners can attend, speak, or vote – so that counts you out!

The ruling council decides what will be discussed at an assembly. Citizens at the assembly then discuss, for example, whether to go to war, build new ships, or change the law. The citizens also decide who should be part of the ruling council.

Athens is unusual as most city-states at this time are ruled by a king or a small group of important people. In Sparta, a city-state that is often at war with Athens, they have two kings.

Top Tip

Look for the herald

The herald stands next to the speakers' platform and invites male citizens to speak on whatever is being discussed at the assembly. It's also his job to count the votes. It takes a long time to count up to 6,000 raised hands!

Banished!

About once a year, the male citizens of Athens write the name of a person they want to banish on a piece of pottery called an *ostracon*. This might be because they feel this person is a threat to Athens or they just don't like them. If enough people write the same name, that person is thrown out of the city and is not allowed to return for 10 years!

TIME TO EXERCISE!

As you walk around Athens, you'll notice men and boys disappearing into the three public gymnasia around the city. Each gymnasium offers plenty of space to practice running, long jump, throwing the javelin or discus, or taking part in wrestling or boxing contests. A covered running track runs all around the edge. Why not join in? (Although you are not welcome if you are a girl or a woman.)

Top Tip

Listen in

Teachers and philosophers gather at the gymnasium to discuss ideas and pass on knowledge to their pupils – teenage boys from wealthy families.

Top Tip

Fit and strong

Don't be shocked, but men and boys take off all their clothes to exercise in the nude. The only thing they put on is a layer of olive oil to protect them from dust! Ancient Greeks admire strong, muscly bodies and they also believe it is important to keep fit in case they need to take up their weapons and defend Athens from its enemies.

Take a trip to Olympia

If the Olympic Games are on, make time to travel to Olympia, where the games take place every four years. It will take you several days to travel there from Athens, but you will be safe as all wars stop for the Olympics. You can watch the contests and worship at the Temple of Zeus, as the games are dedicated to him.

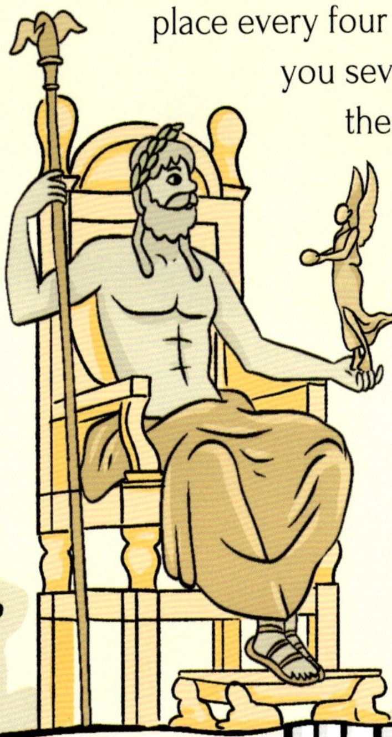

Look out for: keen competitors

The best athletes train for the many sporting competitions held across ancient Greece. If you are lucky, you may catch the Panathenaia, a big sporting festival held in Athens every four years as part of a celebration to honor the goddess Athena. It lasts several days and attracts athletes from across Greece. Winners receive pottery jars filled with olive oil.

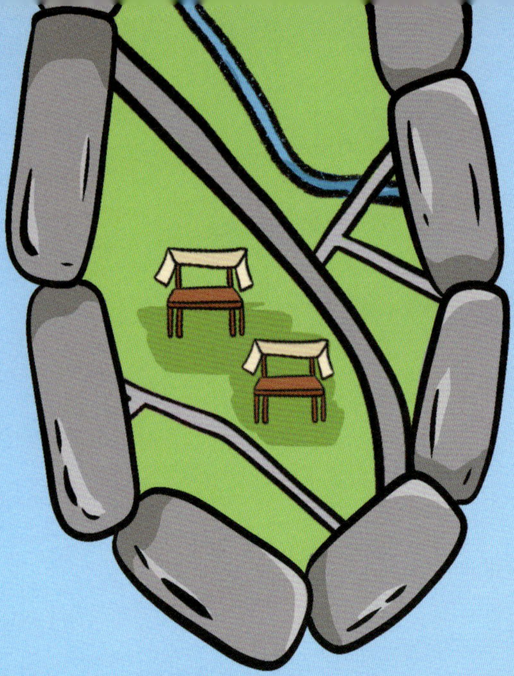

GO SHOPPING

Wander along the streets of Athens and you'll often find they lead you into the agora, a meeting place and shopping spot at the center of Athens. It's a busy place with market stalls and stone buildings. If you want to pick up some souvenirs of your trip, this is the place for you.

Market stalls

Farmers, fishermen, and skilled craftspeople bring their goods to the agora to sell them to the people of Athens. Look out for stall holders selling olives, vegetables, honey, cut flowers, perfume, spices, fish, cheese, hot snacks, jewelry, cloaks, pots, and shoes. Most of the goods are grown or made locally, but some come from far away and were brought to Athens by ship (see page 8).

People for sale

The market for selling enslaved people is in one corner of the agora. You will be horrified, but it is considered quite normal for ancient Greeks to buy, sell, and own people. Some of these people are the children of enslaved people while others became enslaved by being taken prisoner during a war.

Top Tip

Feeling hungry?

The agora is a good place to buy a snack. Bread and olives are a good choice or look around for something else you'd like.

Clever chat

The agora is also a meeting place. Some of the brainiest Athenian writers and philosophers, such as Socrates and Plato, meet here to discuss ideas or talk about what is going on in the city. You may be lucky enough to hear some lively discussions.

VISIT A POTTERY WORKSHOP

While you are at the agora, go to one of the stalls selling pottery and ask whether you can visit the workshop where the pots are made. The potters of Athens are famous for the quality of their red clay pots. Some of the very best pots are bought by merchants who transport them to markets far away from Athens.

Pottery demo

Ask the potter to show you how he makes a pot or vessel.

- He starts by throwing a lump of soft, red clay onto a potter's wheel.
- He spins the round base of the potter's wheel with his hands to get it moving. Then he shapes the clay into a pot with his hands.
- He adds handles.
- He leaves the pot to dry for a while before decorating it by painting a picture or pattern on it.
- When the pot has been fired in a hot oven called a kiln, the picture or pattern appears as red on black (or the other way around).

Top Tip

Spot the trainee

Talk to the potter's son about his training. It doesn't matter if he wants to become a wrestler or a writer – if he is the son of a potter, he'll become a potter too.

Pots for all purposes

The ancient Greeks used pottery pots, vases, jugs, and jars for many purposes. Glance around the workshop and you'll see pots of all shapes and sizes. See if you can spot some of these:

- a kylix – a drinking cup
- a krater – for mixing wine and water
- an amphora – used for transporting or storing foods, such as wine, olive oil, or wheat
- an *oinochoe* – a small jug dipped into a krater to pour wine into a kylix
- a *hydria* – used to transport and store water
- a *lekythos* – for storing olive oil.

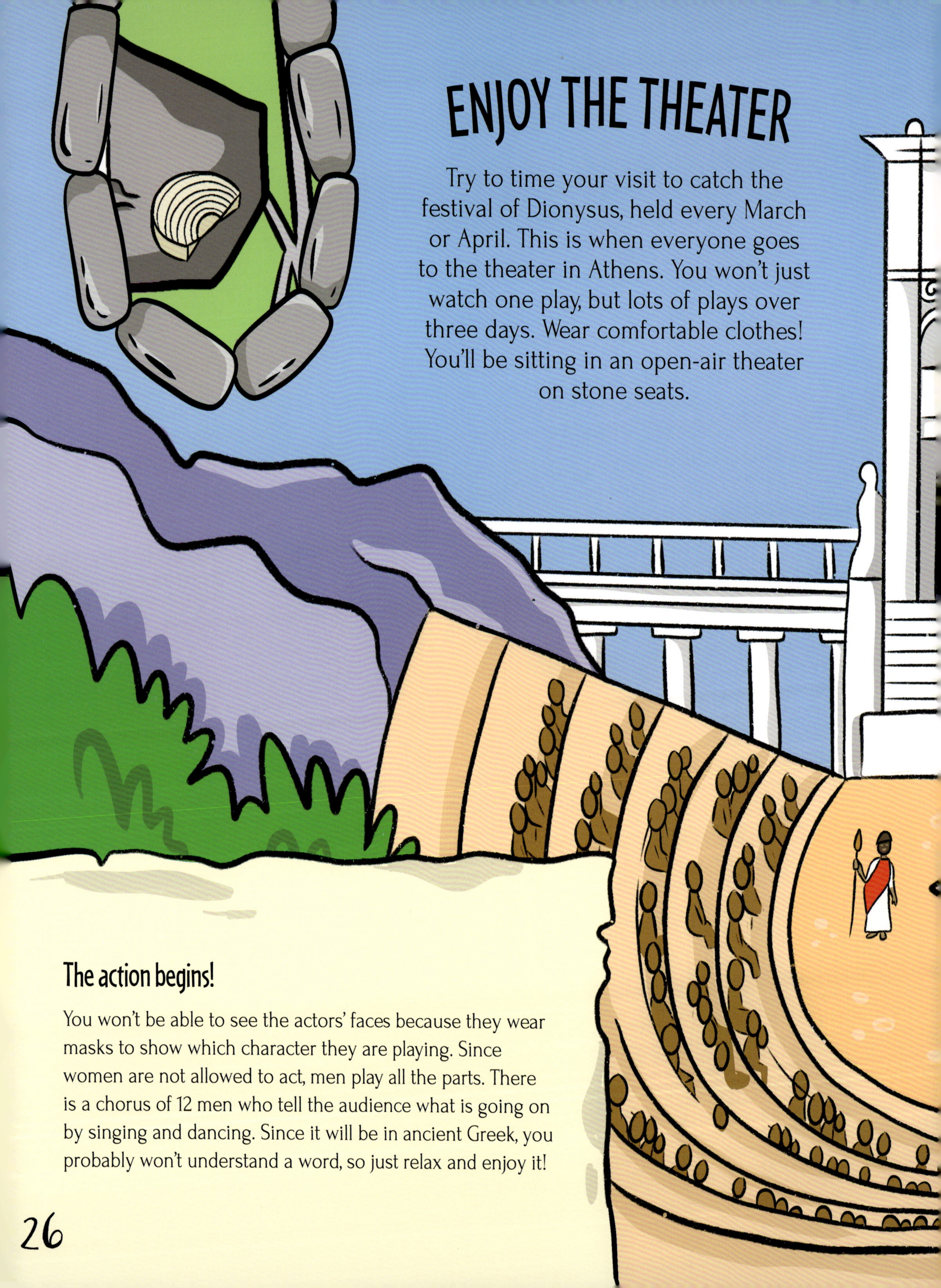

ENJOY THE THEATER

Try to time your visit to catch the festival of Dionysus, held every March or April. This is when everyone goes to the theater in Athens. You won't just watch one play, but lots of plays over three days. Wear comfortable clothes! You'll be sitting in an open-air theater on stone seats.

The action begins!

You won't be able to see the actors' faces because they wear masks to show which character they are playing. Since women are not allowed to act, men play all the parts. There is a chorus of 12 men who tell the audience what is going on by singing and dancing. Since it will be in ancient Greek, you probably won't understand a word, so just relax and enjoy it!

Festival of Dionysus

Dionysus is the god of fertility, pleasure, and wine. His festival lasts five days. It starts with thousands of people dancing through the streets on their way to the theater. There's room for 10,000 people to sit down. If you don't have a ticket, you can watch from a hillside nearby.

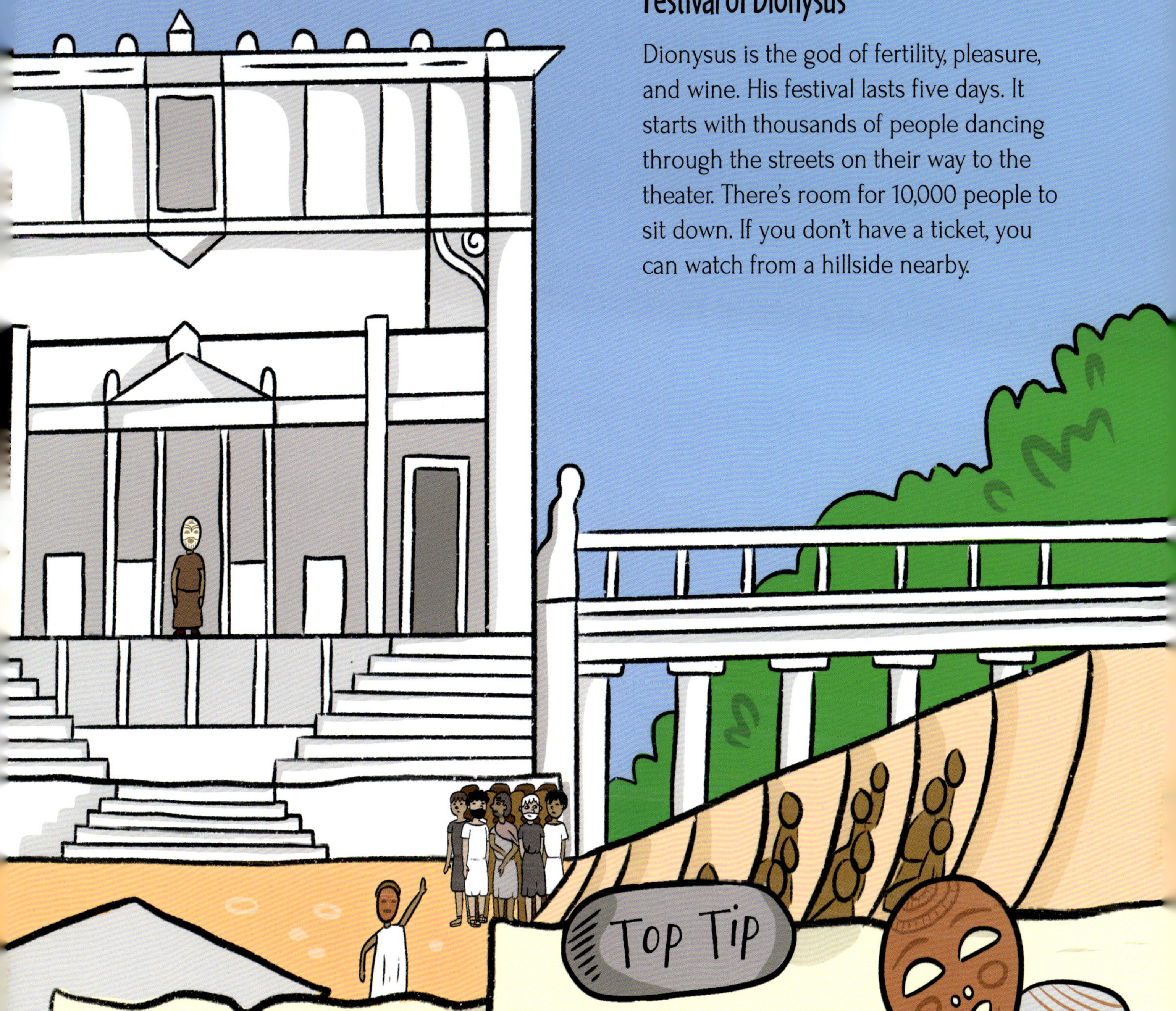

Play contest

All the plays are written by Athens' greatest writers. Every play is new and is entered into a competition. Judges sit near the stage and announce the winner on the final day of the festival.

Do your homework

Amazingly, about 30 tragedies written by ancient Greek playwrights Aeschylus, Sophocles, and Euripides have survived today, as well as 12 comedies by Aristophanes. You could try to find out about them before you leave on your time travels.

VISIT QUICK!

Athens and its citizens have good times and bad times. When you are visiting, Athens is a great and powerful city-state, but there is trouble ahead. A plague will kill thousands of people in Athens in 431 BCE. Then, in 430 BCE, Athens will start fighting a 27-year war with Sparta. Eventually Sparta will defeat Athens in 404 BCE.

Defenders of the city-state

All young men between the ages of 18 and 20 had to be part of the army or navy. Your friend's son is a hoplite – a foot soldier. His family had to buy his armor and weapons, including a bronze helmet, a long spear, a sword, and a heavy, round shield. After two years he can leave, but he will need to keep fit and be ready to fight, should Athens be attacked.

Alexander the Great

Long after your visit, the famous leader, Alexander the Great (356–323 BCE), will create a huge ancient Greek empire called Macedon, stretching from Greece as far as present-day India, Egypt, Persia (Iran), and Bactria (Afghanistan). Greek language and ideas will spread across this empire.

The ancient Romans

Eventually, the ancient Romans will defeat the ancient Greeks at the Battle of Corinth in 146 BCE. However, this won't be the end of Greek ideas, writings, and beliefs. The Romans admired a lot of Greek ideas and adopted them as their own. They renamed some of the Greek gods and goddesses and continued to worship them. They also read Greek plays and other writings, translating them into their own language, Latin, and copying them out many times. Along with surviving objects and buildings, this is why we know so much about the ancient Greeks today.

GLOSSARY

Altar A flat stone or table used for religious worship.

Ancient Roman Someone who lived in Italy, or later the Roman Empire, between the 8th century BCE and CE 476.

Archaeologist Someone who studies history by examining objects, buildings, and ruins from the past.

Banish To force someone to leave their home (village, town, or city) as a punishment.

Bedbug A small insect that feeds on the blood of humans or other animals.

Chamber pot A pot that is kept indoors and is used as a toilet.

City-state A city and its surrounding land, with its own government and ways of life.

Democracy A system of government where those who are allowed to vote have a say in how things are run.

Fertility The ability to produce children.

Frieze On the Parthenon, a band of stone carvings that runs around the top of the outside of the building.

Harbor A place on the coast where boats and ships can safely moor (tie up) and shelter.

Law The set of rules made by a government or society that tells people what they may, or may not, do.

Loom A wooden frame used to weave cloth.

Merchant Someone who buys and sells goods, often transporting them to markets.

Mosaic A pattern made from colored pieces of pottery or stone.

Navy The warships and sailors who fight at sea and defend a country or city-state.

Persian Someone who lived in ancient Persia, now today's Iran.

Philosopher Someone who thinks deeply about the world and how we live in it.

Plague A serious disease that spreads easily from person to person.

Sacred Something that is important to religious people.

Statesman A political leader.

FURTHER INFORMATION

Books

A Question of History: Why Did the Ancient Greeks Ride Elephants into Battle?
Tim Cooke (Wayland, 2022)

Uncover History: Ancient Greece
Rachel Minay (Wayland, 2023)

Websites

Discover more facts and information about ancient Greece at:
www.natgeokids.com/uk/teacher-category/ancient-greeks/

Visit this BBC bitesize website to learn more:
www.bbc.co.uk/bitesize/topics/z87tn39

INDEX

Acropolis 6, 16–18
agora 5–6, 22–25
Alexander the Great 29
andron 11–13
assemblies 18–19
Attica 7

banishment 19
bathrooms 10

children 8, 14–15, 23
clothing 14–16, 21–22
Corinth 4, 29
council 18

democracy 18

enslaved people 8, 10, 12, 15, 18, 23
Erechtheion 16–17

festivals 21, 26–27
food 5, 8, 13, 15, 22–23, 25

goddesses 7, 10, 16–17, 21, 29
gods 7, 9–10, 21, 26–27, 29
gymnasium 14, 20
gynaikon 10, 14–15

harbor 6–9
homes 6, 10–15

krater 12, 24–25
kylix 12–13, 24–25

market see *agora*
merchants 8, 24

Olympia 4, 21
Olympic Games 21

Panathenaia 21
Parthenon 6, 16–17
Pericles 7
philosophers 20, 23
Piraeus 6, 8–9, 11
Plato 23
Pnyx 6, 18–19
pottery 8, 19, 21, 24–25

Romans, ancient 7, 29

Socrates 23
soldiers 28
Sparta 4, 15, 18, 28
spinning 14–15
symposium 12–13

temples 9, 16–17, 21
theater 6, 26–27
toys 14
trireme 9
tunic 14

voting 15, 18–19

war 7–8, 16, 18, 21, 23, 28
weaving 14–15